ARPI MUERWALD AMA*RYJLLA is a recognized healer, channel and spiritual teacher. Ama*Ryjlla is her channeled spiritual name.

Arpi was born on 6 January 1957 in Istanbul, Turkey, of Armenian heritage. She immigrated with her parents to the USA (Detroit, Michigan) in 1959. As a member of a musical family, her talent for music was strongly supported. As a young child, she began playing cello, often joining her renowned cousins in family chamber music. She later attended college at the Eastman School of Music in Rochester, NY, followed by the Juilliard School of Music in New York. During this time she won several competitions and awards.

After marrying a Viennese cellist and moving to Austria, where she had two children and continued playing cello professionally, she discovered her medial talents and began developing her own style of channelings.

Her first of a series of channeled transmissions, a new healing method using combined geometrical forms called 'Metahologramme®', was the inspiration for two books. Written in German, *Metatron Band I* and *Metatron Arbeitsbuch I* were best sellers in many New Age bookstores for several years.

Ama*Ryjlla currently resides in Klosterneuburg, Austria, where she maintains a private teaching and healing practice. Her numerous clients come from various German-speaking countries. As the founder of 'Metahologramme®', she conducts workshops in Austria, where she teaches this useful and effective method.

For further information about Ama*Ryjlla's work, please see her web site: www.amaryjlla.com

*I thank you that this book is
held free from distortion
in all time and space.*

Prayers of Manifestation

creating reality with words

AMA*RYJLLA

WATKINS PUBLISHING
LONDON

This edition first published in the UK and USA 2013 by
Watkins Publishing Ltd, Sixth Floor,
75 Wells Street, London W1T 3QH

A member of Osprey Group

1 3 5 7 9 10 8 6 4 2

Typeset by Bookcraft Ltd, Stroud, Gloucestershire
Printed and bound in China by Imago

A CIP record for this book is available from the British Library

ISBN: 978-1-78028-547-4

www.watkinspublishing.co.uk

Distributed in the USA and Canada by Sterling Publishing Co., Inc.
387 Park Avenue South, New York, NY 10016-8810

For information about custom editions, special sales, premium and
corporate purchases, please contact Sterling Special Sales
Department at 800-805-5489 or specialsales@sterlingpub.com

Contents

Contents

INTRODUCTION

*T*he voice said to me 'now you are ready'. It was in English. It seemed so real, although I had never heard English during a channeling before. I was working with my client in vibrational healing mode, which means that he was not literally in front of me. I had projected into his realm of existence in order to release his current blockages.

I knew the voice was Ar*Ju*Na, since I had met him before, a twelfth-dimensional light entity that was obviously strongly connected to me. His voice was clear, as if we were speaking on the telephone. His message was a mystery to me. I couldn't imagine what could be of such value und use in these days, where so many channeling books were being written. Many channels had spoken before me. What could possibly be new?

He told me to record his exact words or write them down immediately, since they would be coded healing frequencies, and it was critical that I would write them exactly as he gave them to me. The reason I would have to write in English was that in Austria all frequencies were already occupied by German-speaking channels and it was necessary to find a clear connection.

Without me asking any questions, he went on and on about how it would be. In all my previous channelings, I had to ask specific questions in order to receive any appropriate answers. I had often looked for answers that were essential in helping my clients, who in the meantime were coming to me with complex problems and illnesses. As it always was, every expansion in my knowledge through my channeling research attracted new clients that had exactly that specific condition. I knew in advance that many people would call me within the next few days, and they would need to know and profit from exactly the information I had newly received.

This time it was different. He said I would stop everything I was doing, everything I had researched, everything I had developed over years of hard work and experimentation. He said I would have to be courageous. I was stunned and slightly confused.

As my mind began to realize what I was hearing, I was at first not able to believe what I heard. It must be some nasty negative entity that wants to keep me from doing my work, I thought. Where would I find the time for such a project? Why me, since I had already dedicated myself to a project of healing with geometry, had already written books, held seminars, trained dedicated healers, attracted clients with a wide variety of complex situations that I could explore, to try my new-found methods? I was enjoying my life. I had found my ulti-mate goal, or so I thought. What could be so special that I would have to stop doing what I had built up, day and night? I felt myself very privileged, endowed with many gifts and was happy to be and to work. Why change all that?

The manifesting prayers I have documented were the answer I received.

MESSAGE FROM A LIGHT ENTITY NAMED AR*JU*NA

I am Ar*Ju*Na. I send you my golden blue crystal ray of light, so that we may blend and be one for this channeling experience. I come from a high plane of existence called the twelfth plane. Here we are bathed in an overwhelming glow of light. It would not be possible for you to see my hues of existence; I have changed our form in order to be visible to you and communicate with you at this time.

It is our job to watch over you and protect you in your strong will of desire to live on the earth plane. Life on the earth as you know it is your focus at this moment of now. You have chosen it as your mainstream of independent ray, with which you create 'reality', as such, in that which you think to be true. Your reality is made up of different experiences out of your past and your future, put together from many memories, like colors on a painting, just as you have chosen the motives and colors distinctly to fit your particular desire of reality. Within this ray of existence, you have chosen for certain events to happen, whereas other events you have not chosen.

You live your life like a musician, playing the notes in a composition, however interpreting them in your own fashion, sometimes more at liberty, sometimes sharp and distinct, sometimes slower and more melodious. We are here to guide you to play these notes from your sheet of music, more or less how you have chosen the piece you will be playing. So as it is planned, it is the most wonderful song that you will play on earth. The hesitation or the wrong notes, with which you sometimes play, when you don't tune in to the harmony of the song as intended, depends on you. Only you can make this song so distinctly yours and as colorful as your soul in its entirety.

You have put a puzzle together many times and you know how it feels to hold the pieces in your hands. Each piece is only a fraction of that puzzle, so that you don't have a chance to see the whole puzzle before it is completed. Each piece is valuable, for if you left it out you would be missing an essential element. The order in which you fit them together is up to you. After adding several pieces you can see more of a connection, a theme, even a part of the picture, with which you associate something you have known before.

It is important that you can put these analogies into the context I have intended, to understand the complete picture I want to show you in this given moment, in this time and space. Similar to this, there are a vast number of pictures of your existence, in an endless amount of planes, constantly creating new realities, and living many, many more varieties of yourself. Your recollections of these other lives are separated through thin membranes which prevent you from being over-whelmed and keep your conscious focus on this earth plane. We call them 'positive blockages', which we will be explaining later in this book.

The other planes in which you unconsciously exist do not require your direct attention at this given now. They will be more and more relevant, as your consciousness grows to the width and depth that is necessary to reach and integrate the many other consciousnesses of your-self. This will begin to happen in the near future. It is however intended and we will of course support you in dealing with it as it comes.

I, Ar*Ju*Na, and many others have agreed to guide you and see that you are constantly reminded of the path that you have chosen. None the less, it is a path you can leave and come back to, time after time.

It is however a time in our universe, where applica-tion and dedication to the most direct route towards development reduce suffering and pain. Frequently it is fear and doubt that inhibit you and influence you to lose your view of the bigger picture. As the earth is rapidly accelerating in frequency and stability, acquiring clear perception is the key in coping with the inevitable leaps of change in this now and the following next future.

Where are you going after this earth experience? Many of you will go on to other planes of existence, that you have already chosen, to find the adventures that you would like to repeat and relive on other planes, with other properties and other possibilities. Your learning and experiencing will continue, as you augment and unfold your multiple self. As the universe evolves, you will infinitely evolve and expand to a 'whole'. At a very high level of evolution, a frequency unavailable to you now, all deficiency, all imperfection, will cease to exist. Until then you will continuously learn to create your most unique and godlike self, in all there is. There is no end.

The earth experience at this time is a very special one. The very narrow frequency range of 'reality' that is available to you allows an intense focus, with which you can discover yourself in depth and identify your true self. This possibility does not exist in higher planes of existence. In this reality you can live the essence of a program, in a short time span.

The lessons you can take here are quite repetitive compared to other planes. The main program module offered on earth is the subject of relationships. You savor relationships to people, to other living beings and to material objects, in depth and clarity, which you repeat in various constellations again and again, until you have developed an inner sense of the subtlety of expression between you and all that is, in a vast amount of varieties, in every personal contact you make.

We are here with you, yet many of you cannot feel our presence or at least not the full capacity of our presence. It is our intention to be able to communicate with you in your future on a much easier level of expression, similar to your relationship to others around you, although much finer and more detailed. We are working on every possible form of inspiration, to encourage you to train yourself to hear us more clearly every day. While engaging in contemplation, meditating, having religious experiences, spending time in nature, listening to elevating music, etc. you are becoming more and more open and sensitive to our vibrations. Our future together without pain and insecurity is inevitable.

FOCUSING
MIND POWER

*W*ords can be devastating, cruel, humiliating or empowering. You have experienced that repeatedly on a daily basis. But wouldn't it be elevating and fulfilling to speak the language of universal power, like a magic formula. Your words would reach 'God' and materialize the miracles that you are hoping for. This book is about all of that. It's about finding your inner connection to your soul, your spirit guides, your divine hierarchy, your godlike potential, in other words, your own mind power.

In effect, there are many reasons for living and being less than the miracle you are, as a God-born being. Not only have you cut yourself apart from your origin, in order to learn and grow, you have also inflicted repeated situations of pain and guilt upon yourself. Your subtle body is torn and dull with centuries of an unexplainable chain of events, unless you recognize and realize the perspective of all time-chain energy.

Time is endless, but for us to live each experience to the fullest, we create a chain of reactions that determine our journey within all that is. While limiting our power and focusing our energy to our weakest extensions, the third- and fourth-dimensional reality, and encouraging these to develop, we merge with our God self.

It is not yet 'time' to be invincible. Your soul yearns for:

- the cleansing of all negative programs of victimhood
- balancing male and female aspects
- achieving perfect polarity
- eliminating third- and fourth-dimensional manipulative structures
- the expansion of the Universal Heart
- oneness with the Universal Heart
- the knowledge of existence, outside of the limited personality
- the connection with all your planes of existence
- the connection with other light beings
- the joy of being.

Your Soul is Craving to Live its Purpose

What is the purpose of your life? What is your soul's purpose? Are you on the right track to living your higher purpose? How do you know? How can you develop your highest potential? These are some of the important questions that arise during your life on this earth plane.

The truthful answers to all questions are multidimensional. That means, there are an infinite amount of different truths. That is why the truth and the answers to your questions can only be individually found. The answers you seek depend on the perspective from which you are looking. In every given moment, the truth is the reality that you have created for yourself. It is up to you to change your truth und therefore your reality.

Each one of us is the reality of God's essence in the very now. The reason it is important to understand every aspect of this 'truth' is that in understanding, we mobilize the inner essence of the mind. Mind is universal – it connects us to the universe, which we can access, given that we are able to understand the rules and regulations for tapping into it.

To understand the overall picture and broader truth of your personal 'history and reaction chain', you have to be fully connected to the monad, the origin of your journey, the beginning of your time-reaction-chain. This is where you began to limit and chastise yourself for 'leaving home'. This is the source of the 'original sin'. It is the first guilt we have taken upon ourselves for having to leave the comfort and support of unlimited happiness (at home with 'God') into the boundaries of hopelessness and sorrow – the illusion of leaving home.

As you go along on your journey, alone and 'without source', you gather one experience after another of disappointment and despair, until you identify yourself with fear, disconnection and powerlessness. This induces a chain of reactions, by the law of attraction, which lead you through a countless number of realities in suffering, torment and unworthiness. This makes you grow and evolve in unimaginable ways, to experience the richness of every aspect of your being.

You are who you are now, because of your 'richness' of experience, although you are tired and held back with the weight of the 'past'. Your life is good, but it is hard. Your life is rewarding but not light and easy. You are confronted daily with challenges that are mostly unmanageable – in your partnership and communication with others, in your feeling of achievement and fulfillment of purpose, in your health issues. Your energy is spent battling and maneuvering.

You can elevate yourself to your power of mind – begin now. Disconnect yourself from the frequency of pain and suffering.

THE POWER OF WORDS: 'THE WORD SHALL LIGHT THE WAY'

*W*e are all composed of infinite frequencies of energy in various denser and higher ranges. A denser form of energy for instance is what our physical body consists of. The higher frequencies, like the emotional or mental bodies can only be seen by people with highly developed sensitive skills. The aura is made up of a vast amount of different higher frequencies, depending on the function of the particular layer.

Cymatics is a special process that helps prove that the vibrations of spoken words can take geometric forms. Words hold the power of focus and intention. 'I thank you that it is so, now' is the most powerful manifestation in this universe. It contains the unwavering conviction of your belief. Depending on the frequency this thought is sent on (intensity of conviction) and the direction that it is sent in (the focus), this thought can strongly influence a situation or person in a supporting or defeating way. The frequency or intensity of conviction is accurately correspondent to the awareness and degree of spiritual maturity of the person sending out the manifestation.

In order to focus the manifestation, practice and training over a longer period of time is required. The mere intention of the words you send is not yet sufficient. Your thought must be higher-dimensional, in other words, sent with higher vibrations than all other frequencies around you to fully resonate in the highest possible intensity of power.

All healing methods have one principle in common: to bring order into chaos. Correctly chosen, words can ultimately describe the wholeness, the oneness and knowingness within you, which envelop the unity between you and your highest potential. When you are one with your highest self in focus, clarity and intention, your manifestation has immense power. Your words can bring forth healing power in all aspects of your life.

Generally, as you know, a choice of words and the combination of words in a sentence are used for different purposes, for instance poems, literature or personal expression. You want to explore and activate a new combination of words, using the power of focus and intent, to manifest healing in every area of problems and issues concerning your life as an earth being. Words, in form of the given prayers, will be used intentionally as a therapeutic tool.

Each word has its own frequency. To recognize the difference in the frequency of words, *feel* the following frequencies. Notice the dynamic difference that escalates more and more with each further sentence.

I hope it is so
I think it is so
I imagine it is so
I believe that it is so
I want it to be so
I deserve it to be so
I'm sure that it is so
I know that it is so.

A further example would be:

Please help me
Please support me
Please make it so
Please let me feel it to be so
Please let it be so
Thank you that it is so, now.

Shaping Your Future
with Words

S poken words and thoughts can have an unimaginable power of creating your destiny. Spoken with conviction, emotion and 'knowingness', they can change your deep inner feelings of unworthiness and give you the chance to clean your slate of unwanted residue. Those are the feelings that weigh you down, that hold you back from being one with yourself, your potential and the forces in this universe.

Words can keep you in constant restriction or in resistance with yourself and others. They can keep you bound to thoughts of imperfection, intolerance, unhappiness, etc. These are the feelings that project out to others and create misunderstandings of who you are and what your intention is. These are the beliefs that repeatedly magnetize the same unsatisfactory situation, making it practically impossible to change the outcome of your efforts.

Why can words have such a strong hold on our energy? How can they sabotage our capacity to be our perfect selves and influence the outcome of our daily and future experiences?

Words express your inner convictions or non-convictions, the clearness or unclearness of your intention, your feelings and your desires. With words you can mobilize the power of the entire universe. Isn't that a scary thought? Are most of your thoughts and therefore your words unclear? Are they about lack in every situation you see, hear and feel?

How much power do your words have and how can you use them as a tool? Does that make you a selfish being, only looking for personal gain? How does it fit the greater picture of changes that are happening all around us? Why is it important to understand the outcome of your thoughts?

The frequencies with which you send your thoughts into the universe match your momentary awareness. You are provided the opportunity to use your words recklessly, thoughtlessly, etc. for many moments of existence, in order to make the experience of lacking.

As more and more portals are opening, light is pouring into this earth system; the magnetic properties of the poles are changing, a new now is being created in every minute. Your thoughts are changing. Your feelings are changing; your fears, your 'negative' convictions and deepest contradictions are confronting you more than ever before. It is a cleansing process that has begun in a subtle way, over many years, growing in intensity, growing in accuracy, showing us our power or lack of power over our lives more precisely, with every new now.

Imagine how you could use your words to change your entire life now. Fortunately you couldn't. Not without learning to identify yourself with your thoughts. Immediately your unexpected fears would arise, letting you feel inadequate, helpless and uncomfortable. It would be impossible to adjust yourself to your new life-style, no matter how much you wished for it in the past. Your mind needs time to access and re-evaluate, time to understand and incorporate changes which induce new situations.

You know what it's like trying to see things positively and failing after many attempts. When you force yourself to think positively, sometimes the opposite occurs. You can't stop thinking of: ifs, buts and why nots. Your ego and intellect will not believe you and your subconscious will not take on the change. The real changes happen if and when you involve all parts of your existence. The obvious ones are your subconscious, ego, reason ... but also your physical body's consciousness. YOU are infinite. In every incarnation where you manifest yourself, you never cease to exist. In all planes of your existence you create new blockages through negative experiences. If you are clearly able to create your desires into reality, it is only so because you have released all resistance to those desires in ALL parts of your existence.

Your 'higher' dimensions have their consciousness and own 'personality'. They are your higher self, your soul, your oversoul, your monad ... and all the higher dimensions of your divine hierarchy, up to the very moment of your individual birth into existence. It is essential that your whole existence in every plane and dimension is willing and prepared to undergo the changes. All planes must be asked for permission and thanked for their dedication and cooperation. Otherwise they would most likely resist and make it impossible to move ahead. The power and intensity of purpose that you need to evoke change can only be channeled through the vastness of your entirety.

Of course there are special situations that have to be accepted and even trusted. In some cases, our whole soul entity has another plan for us in store. Since we are used to making decisions with a very old friend and habit, the ego, our motives are often seen from a much smaller perspective. The many pieces of the puzzle that would be needed in order to fully comprehend the meaning of our existence are hidden to us. We feel that we cannot realize our dreams and act on false assumptions. Our life experiences will be based on the wrong context and will lead us to act against our higher goals.

After several attempts from our highest aspects of being to lead us to success and happiness, the body 'decides' to get ill and die, in order to start all over again. Our soul is not always born for the sole purpose of living a full life. Sometimes the whole picture can only be seen from a 'non-living', 'between lives' situation. For those of you that do not believe in reincarnation, please consider the following:

You consist of dense energy. The laws of physics tell us that energy cannot be eliminated; it can only change its form. One could say, nature never wastes or loses life experiences, for life experience is produced for the profound purpose of expansion. Your existing being is constantly growing and expanding in order to profit from this experience. One lifetime is a very short and inadequate time span for this process to be completed.

Another very important concept that should be considered before one begins to project manifestation is the principle of bipolarity. Universal scientific and also spiritual principles and laws, which help us to understand patterns, repetitions and connections in this reality, have been discovered over centuries. Pertaining to spiritual growth, frequencies of light and darkness can be explained as opposites, which are necessary for the expansion of the whole. However within darkness itself, there are infinite frequencies that define a vast difference of levels between, for instance, unawareness and manipulation. Naturally and fortunately there also exists an unimaginable amount of light frequencies that separate us from our full power of source energy.

Defined by the law of attraction, the higher we develop our light frequencies, the more we attract the higher and more subtle energies of manipulation. To be fully healed from all discrepancies in one's universal highest truth, self and mind, it is necessary to transform all subtle and less subtle forms of manipulation.

The subjects that will especially be treated are:

- Ultimate relationships
- Fulfilling potential
- Flow of wealth and happiness
- Health and well-being
- Healing the heart and emotions
- Spiritual growth
- Developing a higher consciousness
- Clearing your energy fields of residue and the influences of black magic.

THE DIFFERENCE BETWEEN RESISTANCE AND NEGATIVE OR POSITIVE BLOCKAGES

*B*efore your words can be influential or have the ultimate power of frequency, the greater percentage of resistance should be removed. By resistance, I don't mean blockages. Resistance begins in your personal reality, as a reaction to continual blockages. It simply means that after repeated experiences of lack, fear and other demeaning emotions, you develop a resistance to freedom from fear, contentment and joy. The amounts of negative experiences add up to such a barrier that you lose faith in your potential to being happy. The more often you experience the hard side of life the more you lose your feeling of being nurtured and cared for by the universe. In other words, you lose your essential 'godliness', the natural knowingness of freedom, joy and power of source.

Through your millions of years of existence and consistency of existence in thousands of other planes, your system is full of blockages with which you associate your personality. Your 'personality' is nothing more or less than your reactions to all the negative and positive experiences of each and every moment of your existence. You most likely protest against this thought and claim that your personality is the individual part of yourself and that giving it up would mean that you are like everyone else. Unfortunately, this conviction is the barrier that keeps you from discovering your 'godlike' self. This belief is caused by your deepest fears of losing yourself, losing your life's orientation, not knowing who you are, in short, giving up your ego.

But who are you really? Are you only the sum of all your negative and positive experiences and your reactions to them? Or do you have the potential to be more? Isn't it our decisions that make us who we are and how we differ from others? Your soul is unique. If you choose to be the expression of your soul, you are irreplaceable!

It is your conviction and view of yourself that allow no other possibilities. You trap yourself daily in barriers of well-ordered structures, which help you to survive while being protected from your deepest fears. Any wavering of these barriers feels dangerous or unreasonable.

Your thoughts help you to decide what action should be taken. Based on what you've experienced in this life (which is definitely not the whole picture), your fears, or what others say to you or about you, you will be influenced. You repeatedly subconsciously manifest your own convictions of the lack of your abilities. You miss out on the opportunities that would make your life wonderful and elevating.

CREATING REALITY WITH PRAYERS OF MANIFESTATION

*T*he following prayers have been created in the twelfth plane of existence in order to open and elevate your frequency of awareness. In doing so, your frequency and therefore your power to manifest will grow exponentially. The following meditation will activate and extend your frequency each time during this work.

Please read this before starting!

Do not use all prayers at once. Select a few of your priorities and work on them until some change occurs. Each prayer will activate the release of resistance against the specific subject. If you have particularly much resistance, you will begin to change your opinions, feelings, convictions and perspective until you develop your new truth. The intensity of the change could cause your subtle bodies to tear. Torn subtle bodies can result in tiredness, an aching head and sore throat. In case you have manifested too many prayers in too short a time and you feel physically run down or emotionally upset, cleanse your auric field. Use the preparation prayers to help you get back into balance. Since excessive application can also attract negative energies or entities (when your bodies are torn, they are not compact and therefore prone to infliction), it is advisable to begin with only one or two manifestation prayers. Should you attract them, please use the prayers in 'Disconnecting Dark Entities' (pages 205–223) to eliminate these blockages before working further.

Depending on how blocked you are, you will most likely undergo a process. The intensity of the process should not exceed your capacity to integrate the new changes into your life. The preparation prayers can be used more often in order to keep your auric field in balance.

SIMPLE GUIDELINES

Now that you have read the background information and have understood the purpose and potential of the following prayers, please take time to acquire a secure basis by using the following exercises:

- A meditation to activate your higher frequency
- Connecting with your heart energy
- Connecting to your spirit and soul.

Next, the 'Preparation Prayers' (pages 49–65) will help you to activate maximum energy for the manifestations you have chosen. They should also be utilized in the following weeks after manifesting a prayer to help you keep in balance and bring on the changes in your daily life.

Further, the prayers in 'Expansion of Spirit and Soul' (pages 67–97) are essential in activating soul energy. They help you to increase the connection to your highest potential while elevating your spiritual growth. Spiritual growth is the ultimate tool in manifesting without violating universal laws. The prayers in this section should be used regularly, in combination with the prayer you have chosen to manifest from the following chapters.

Choose one or two prayers that you would like to manifest. You can repeat the chosen prayers as often as you feel is good and necessary, until you have received the results. It is helpful to write a few notes documenting your life situation that you would like to change before beginning to manifest. When the changes occur, one quickly tends to forget the initial circumstances.

To manifest, connect yourself to your highest God presence using 'A Meditation to Activate your Higher Frequency'. Recite the prayers, addressing them to your divine hierarchy and chosen light entity. Observe how you feel in the following weeks.

Make sure you are mostly feeling positive and good. If not, use the prayers in 'Preparation Prayers' (pages 49–65) and 'Disconnecting Dark Entities' (pages 205–223).

Finally, we wish you much success in achieving joy and happiness while living your highest godlike potential.

Ar*Ju*Na and Ama*Ryjlla

A MEDITATION TO ACTIVATE YOUR HIGHER FREQUENCY

With each repetition of this meditation, you will clear and strengthen your connection to your universal self. The frequency of your subtle bodies will elevate.

Sit or lie in a comfortable position. Focus on your breathing for a while, until you feel fully relaxed. If thoughts come into your mind, send them on without giving them any attention.

Use the following 'commands' to guide your mind into the twelfth plane of existence.

I am one with my highest God presence.

Feel, see or know the presence through your perception. If you have never trained yourself to refine your awareness, don't be afraid to begin. Cognition must be practiced in order to be used as a tool of information and communication.

Let yourself glide, beginning from this third plane of existence in which you are focused during this lifetime and through the higher planes until you have reached the twelfth plane. On the way up do not look around you or get involved with these other planes. In the twelfth plane you will feel as if all your burdens are gone. This is temporary of course, since you will have to come back to your everyday consciousness when you are finished with manifesting. If you feel confidence and love for the universe and all living beings, you have reached the twelfth plane. If not, don't worry, in time you will. Until then your persistency will be rewarded.

Thank the universal light that you are connected for the duration that is necessary to manifest your chosen prayers.

In order to set the process of manifestation in motion, 'read' the prayers silently or aloud, depending on which variation you feel the most comfortable with. Recite the prayers with love and conviction while focusing on one of the following entities. Choose them in accordance with your deep beliefs since they will work the best for you.

- God
- Universal Light/Universal Truth/All That Is
- Your Spirit Guides
- Your Guardian Angels
- Or others, according to your beliefs.

After you are finished, please take some deep breaths, ground yourself with the center of the earth and balance your electromagnetic impulses and fields by using the 'command':

Thank you that I am completely grounded
with the center of the earth and that my
electro magnetic feilds are perfectly balanced.

'God' represents the highest form of existence. Please feel free to substitute the name of your personal choice.

CONNECTING WITH YOUR HEART ENERGY

Prayers have to come from your heart, in order to be fully activated. Concentrate on your heart and feel the richness and joy of your feelings and intentions. As you do this, you will automatically smile.

Some of you may be blocked to the deeper feelings of your heart. In this case, remember the most wonderful thing that ever happened to you. Spend a few minutes feeling this experience again. Feel how your body and then your heart react to these feelings. These are the vibrations you need, to give your prayer the power to succeed. The power you project is a combination of the prayer and your inner conviction.

When you fully apply your inner yearning to the prayer you have chosen to manifest, you will feel the intense frequency in several parts of your body. Your body will become one with your words and your words will elevate your being to a frequency of knowingness. You will identify yourself with your prayer. This power of certainty is the power of manifestation.

Breathe deeply and observe the reaction of your feelings and thoughts to each prayer. Feel each prayer in

PRAYERS of MANIFESTATION

your body. Observe in which part of your body the sensation resonates. When the prayer is one with your higher self, soul and body, you will produce a vibration that cannot be stopped or diffused. Every word will free your inner potential. Every intense feeling will project your words in all your fields of existence, in all aspects of your universal mind.

Feel the power within you to create alignment and oneness with your universal mind.

There are no particular instructions for using this manifesting tool. However, the affectivity depends on your conviction and feeling while reciting each prayer. If you feel unconvinced or skeptical, there are blockages that separate you from your wished results. In that case, it is important to release these blockages before you have the power to manifest. To do this it is advisable to begin with the prayers in 'Expansion of Spirit and Soul' to resolve all tension. Rely on your perception (not your fears, shortcomings, resolutions, etc.) to recognize if you are ready to manifest the subjects in the other chapters. You might have to repeat the prayer 'Removing Blockages' several times before you can manifest your desired prayer. It all depends on how blocked a certain subject is.

Basically, nothing can go wrong. If your prayers are not manifested you will know soon enough. The prayers in this book achieve results based on the communication between you, your highest light frequency, us and other light entities. We are a group of cosmic healers that have chosen to help you in your endeavor to transcend this earth reality.

We can only help you to heal if you take the responsibility for your feelings, decisions, actions, etc., in short, your part in the evolutionary process of change. We realize that you are not yet qualified to change your subtle bodies, in all unfamiliar structures that are necessary, to eliminate all the blockages to achieve a holistic result and extensive change. You are not all born to be healers, and even then, your knowledge is limited to the current teachings available. There are still many unknown blocked structures that healers will identify and learn about.

Your intention and dedication will be honored. We will respect your wishes in any time and space. By manifesting these prayers, you make a commitment to your soul self and the expansion of your highest consciousness. We will gladly support you in every step of the way.

For each prayer that you choose and get involved with extensively, you will notice the process you undergo and subtle changes will appear. To utilize the full extent of each prayer you may need to repeat it over a longer period of time until you feel that the specific problem has been solved and you have integrated these changes in your life. Your daily life will then reflect the full advantage of these changes. Your confidence and feeling of assurance will convince you that you are letting go of old and taxing beliefs and substituting them with better and more inspiring beliefs.

Your involvement with these manifestations, does not substitute medical, therapeutic or holistic consultations, diagnosis and therapy. Rather, they increase your awareness, raise and balance your energetic frequencies and help you reach a deeper understanding of yourself and your soul's higher purpose. The deeper understanding will help you to integrate the achieved perspective in your life. Finally we hope that the journey you will take will open new doors and inspire your heart to being unconditional.

How blockages reduce frequency

Over thousands of incarnations, you have gathered and stored blockages. The millions of 'negative' experiences or so called 'blockages' are only released when you have reached the final result and understanding of each issue. With each subject your soul has chosen to develop, you will repeatedly experience variations and facets of scenarios that help you to reflect on and process these themes. In your natural state of development you will understand and integrate, life after life, the quintessence of your findings. Almost every living being is bound to these cycles of development.

Each organ, each bone, each cell and every other part of your body has many subtle bodies that extend outside of the physical body. Each blockage you store can be found in one or more layers of several body parts, and is compatible with the subjects that you wish to develop. Unfortunately, it is the 'weight' of these blockages that prevents you from mobilizing your highest possible frequency.

Your body is your instrument. The higher your physical and subtle bodies oscillate, the more powerful your manifestation will be and the more visible changes will occur. The fewer blockages you have stored, the higher your frequencies will be. The following prayers will help you to release your blockages in a well aimed fashion. If you have lived through thousands of extreme and devastating experiences, you will have to be patient and persistent.

It will eventually take several months before you are able to manifest the perfect potential and results of your prayers. For some of you, the prayers will work quickly and easily. Unfortunately there is no X-ray that can tell you which applies to you. Only your efforts and attained results can guide you and give you the information you need to understand your personal history.

In order to increase efficiency it is recommended that you end each prayer with 'Breaking Barriers'. As you will develop and therefore expand your aura quickly, you will need to easily break through layers of barriers, otherwise you might feel tired and 'trapped'. Most barriers of this kind are natural hurdles that you are born with in order to grow one step at a time, without being overwhelmed by each assignment. Some barriers are created by you to protect yourself. This is a subconscious unnecessary reaction which stops you from benefiting from the prayers.

CONNECTING TO YOUR SPIRIT AND SOUL

Many of you are separated from your power to manifest and to integrally heal on all levels. There are several reasons for this, including the blockages that we explained in the previous chapters. It is also necessary to repair the damage, which has occurred over thousands of 'incarnations', before you have full access and communication to your spirit and soul family. The inner creativity and strength, which you can tap into, exists outside of you, in the collective of your highest hierarchy. In other words, if your subconscious, soul and oversoul have been separated, and the pathways between them are blocked, you are limited to only your personal strength. You feel that you have to fight to make your daily life work. Your intuitive choices lead you to complications and strenuous efforts to 'fix the mess'. That is because you are disconnected from the greater power of your soul family. You are alone to manage your life.

Again, to release these blockages, repair damaged pathways and reconnect yourself to your source of power, it may be necessary to repeat the higher manifestation 'Removing Blockages' repeatedly for several weeks.

The time you will need depends on the torn matrices, ethereal bodies, Nadis, etc. that have been caused by the great deal of blockages that you have acquired in your divine axis. Although it takes time for these connections to clear and heal, it is very important to take the time before going on with other manifesting prayers, otherwise nothing will change and you will achieve no results or effective healing.

Another greater barrier that has to be dealt with, for the best manifesting results, is the contrasting resistance, through cosmic laws of duality. All of your cells that are in a 'non-believing' frequency resist healing and are not willing to change, in order to be positively influenced through your manifesting efforts. This resistance can consist of dark entities or even your past lives in other realms that are in resistance or even oppose themselves to God's light and truth. These 'blockages' that prevent good results in manifesting work must be dealt with often on a daily basis. Dark entities are losing their grounds in this extreme time of change. Often, while you go into resonance with negative thoughts and feelings, you can attract negative entities that want to use your energy field or keep you from spiritual growth. Duality originally exists for a higher purpose, to enable us to learn and grow. However, in this level of existence, the programs we have to absolve and transcend are of the lowest duality. Returning to pure light and truth belong to the assignment we have agreed to, before being born to these extreme conditions of 'reality'.

Many of you are here to learn the difference between light and darkness, truth and illusion, love and manipulation, on the pathway to redeeming their godlike self and developing into unity with the universal source of all that is.

RECEIVING THE ULTIMATE INFORMATION

For the ultimate cognitive answers, it is very important to be impartial. Your preferences for one or the other answer, your fears or negative beliefs and blockages in your physical body are all factors that influence and therefore distort your 'information' from the divine source. Since it is not possible to spontaneously dissolve your emotional, mental and physical blockages, to allow a clearer connection, it is advisable to learn to 'switch' your focus into a state of limbo – where there are no preconceived opinions.

You want to be in an immense, endless place of neutrality, a void of all personal interpretation. This abstract but real chamber contains all truths, all unabridged versions of reality, in all time and space. It is an exception, in all planes of existence. The prayer 'Chamber of Neutrality' will help you to find this chamber and benefit from its non-biased quality.

Preparation
Prayers

❧ Dissolving Shock ❧

I thank you that my soul
and all other aspects of being
are now free from shock and stress
throughout all my dimensions and planes.

I thank you that my frequencies of existence
are reorganized and redefined
into perfect formations
of serenity and quiescence
in the core of my self.

I thank you that my inner connection
to all my aspects is restored
and that all my bodies
and my higher bodies are aligned
with my physical, emotional
and mental well-being.

I thank you that my stability
through grounding
with the earth's inner core
is fully established.

I thank you that my aura is
whole and flawless,
according to the principles
of faith and confidence.

I am one with the strength
of universal completeness.

🐚 Breaking Barriers 🐚

I thank you that all barriers
that enclose my expanding freedom of being
are now shed in all frequencies
and dimensions, in every existence
of my universal spirit.

I thank you that each realm
of further expansion
is open to allow room and space,
in the process of my growing reality
of mind consciousness.

I thank you that all illusion
and self-delusion
that may be transformed
in this moment of reality,
in accordance with God's rhythm
of extending abundance and beauty,
are erased.

I thank you for the perception
of perfect clarity
in my ever expanding dimension.

✤ Willing to Change ✤

I thank you that I am now determined
to evoke change, new direction
and new orientation
and therefore willing to accept
each and every step
towards achieving new goals.

I thank you that all fears
of the future and unknown,
of repeated failure and discontent,
of being or feeling overwhelmed,
fear that my ego be destroyed,
and fear of being lost and helpless
are relinquished and give way
to joy and completion.

I thank you that I am one
with my endeavor to grow,
to succeed and to grasp my creative spirit
and to find my ultimate goal
in the glory of my godlike nature.

I thank you that I am supported
at all times of difficulty,
confusion and sadness
that arise through uncertainty
and distrust.

I thank you that I am led
to open new doors
where I am free to live
the essence of my soul.

I am God's enduring quality of strength.

✤ Ultimate Grounding ✤

I thank you that all my fears
of confrontation with life on earth
are diminished and healed,
and that I am free
from anxiety and stress
in earthly matters.

I thank you that my mind and being
are willing to let go
of pain and grief that still prevail
in my experience of reincarnation.

I thank you that every barrier
is removed, and therefore allow
my fullest connection
to the earth's core of security,
clarity and stability.

I thank you that blockages
in my lower body are minimized
to allow a steady growing
love and compassion
for the earth's beauty
and nobel spirit.

I thank you that all fear and anguish
in my past, present and future
are healed and reconciled
and that I am willing to live
in joy and peace.

I thank you that I am in perfect balance
in the cosmic constellation
of all planets, suns and moons
and that every structure in my body
is attuned to perfect polarity.

I thank you that all blockages
in my hips, thighs and feet
that prevent my connection
to the physical reality of life
are dissolved.

I thank you that I am able
to fully understand and appreciate
the gift of life on earth.

I am bestowed with the earth's love of life.

❧ Removing Blockages ❧

I thank you that all blockages
in all frequencies, time and space
that are in resistance
with the wondrous healing power
of my highest God and universe
are diminished and released
in order to allow
my perfect healing process.

I thank you that my physical,
emotional, mental and spiritual
systems and structures
are cleared of all retained memory
that keep me attached
to endless and repetitive
pain and suffering.

I thank you that I am now void
of every past, present
and future destruction
in every cell of my existence
that is allowed and fitting
in this time of redemption
to the subject of: —

I thank you that all causes of discord
in every plane of my existence,
that are allowed to be
released at this time,
are now neutralized and released.

I thank you that I am free
of the cycle of suffering in this subject
and therefore able to manifest
my new, fulfilling and glorious
reality of God's perfection.

I thank you that my mind,
body structures and systems,
and my personality are realigned
in accordance and willing
to discharge any resistance
and restriction that may interfere
with the ultimate release
of ill health, unhappiness
and distortion.

I am God's loving spirit, body and soul.

✿ Clearing Residual Energy ✿

I thank you that every foreign
emotional, mental and spiritual restriction
that I have attracted
from surrounding bodies of energy,
that are now clogging my auric fields,
are transformed and released
into the infinite expanding light.

I thank you that the weight
of pity and burden of responsibility
for others' emotions and thoughts
are released.

I thank you that all magnetic pull
of residual energy is nullified
through the healing of self-blame.

I am the pure thought of I am.

✑ Chamber of Neutrality ✑

I thank you God
that I am relaxed and safe
in every moment now.

I thank you that I am in oneness,
faith and harmony
with universal wisdom.

I thank you that I glide
easily and effortlessly
to the plane of neutrality,
void of emotions, thoughts
and physical reality.

I thank you that I am able to observe,
collect and remember
all information that I receive,
free of illusion, wishful thinking,
personal judgment and opinion.

I thank you that I find now every
answer that I truly seek from my
heart and highest soul,
and that the answers and questions
are the true expression and creativity
of my limitless being.

I thank you for the perfect access
that allows me to achieve relativity
and stay free of all manipulation
through the undermining intent
of my ego-self.

I thank you that my ego is at peace
and willing to understand,
allow and accept the divine answer
on my search for truth.

Thank you.

✤ Trusting God and the Universe ✤

I thank you for the vast, infinite
and open horizon
of my heart, soul and mind
that open every door
and widen every path
to the limitless power of trust.

I thank you that all
my bodies are connected
to the flow of expansion
in all planes of knowing faith.

I thank you that my changing reality
is based on the flowing impulses
of God's wisdom
in every realm of my existence.

I thank you that I feel at home
secure and protected
in God's universal light
and that my unwavering focus is tuned
to the purest conviction
of God's inner truth.

I thank you that my cells are clear
of mistrust, abuse and powerlessness
and willing to accept
the lightness and vigor
of well-being and knowing calm.

I thank you that every thought,
feeling and decision
is matched to my mirror of wisdom
and the unfailing security
of God's infinite commitment.

I thank you that I am free
of all barriers that bind me
and minimize my godlike being.

I thank you that my potential to trust
is empowered
with God's passion and grace.

I thank you that my yearning
for joy and fearlessness
is elevated through
God's helping hand.

I thank you that my striving
for peace and trust
is encouraged through God's strong
and just cause.

I thank you that my potential
to be the perfect expression of my soul
and the highest capacity of my mind
is in unity with God's infinite harmony.

I am expression of God's soul.

Expansion
of
Spirit and Soul

❦ Achieving Clarity ❦

I thank you that my thoughts and feelings
are cleared of all distortion and distraction.

I thank you that my heart and mind
are aligned and profoundly connected
with my spirit and soul,
to fully receive divine
communication and truth.

I thank you that all messages
from my highest planes
are clearly transmitted
so that I may fully understand them
and apply them as they are meant for me.

I thank you that all ties
to my spirit guides and guardian angels
are strengthened to comply with
the perfect convictions
of my highest sentient being.

I thank you that all received information
is in accordance
with my divine path,
light and truth.

I am in clarity and knowledge
of the sustaining light
of my infinite well-being.

Recreating Justice:
Finding the Just Truth

Believe it or not, there is, in every situation, in every action you take, an ultimate truth. Whenever you feel unjustly treated, this feeling is subjective. In this case it is important to re-evaluate and gain a more objective perspective. Often your ego protects you from being able to do so or your emotions clog your auric field, so that you have no overall point of view.

By manifesting the following prayer you ask to see or feel, without offending your self-esteem, if you have been unjust or if you are the 'victim' of injustice. Take the time that is necessary to repeat the prayer and get clarity in the situation, perhaps over a longer period of time. Whichever answers you find, you are responsible for rebalancing the injustice into justice. The clear position you have achieved will make it easier to do so.

⟅ Recreating Justice ⟆

I thank you that my soul, mind
and personality are one
to recognize, understand and
achieve justice.

I thank you that the laws of reality
are clear to me
and that my yearning
to be free from injustice
determine my efforts to seek the perfect truth
in the purity of God's realm.

I thank you for the alignment
of all dimensions and aspects
that are necessary
to evoke the highest perspective
out of which a new
and unconditional order will emerge.

I thank you that my self perceives
the very core of universal justice
apart from each illusion,
self-protection or self-degradation.

I thank you for my neutral position
to fathom and accept
every aspect of the just truth.

I thank you that justice is in balance
and that I am relieved and released from
the inequality of injustice.

ᓚ Gaining Faith ᓚ

I thank you for the faith
and confidence in my heart,
endlessly growing and expanding
in my cells, my mind and my spirit.

I thank you that my entire being
is perceptive and confident
of trust and reliability
in every facet of my earth reality.

I thank you for the elimination
of fear and all barriers
that prevent self-confidence
and the feeling of security
to encourage and promote
my leap of faith.

I am the freedom of God's knowing
wisdom and expansion of trust.

Thank you.

ℒ Increasing Conviction ℒ

I thank you that I know, feel and seek
with certainty, trust and faith
the irrepressible power of
God's healing and loving being
in the cells of my existence.

I thank you that I am willing
to release all fears
of the consequences of conviction
and that I am ready to apply myself
to the maturity of my complete and unified self.

I thank you that my godlike being
is free to be strong and confident
with the joy and strength of increasing conviction.

◌ Releasing Control ◌

I thank you that all resistance of faith
in my highest self and soul
are healed and dissolved.

I thank you that my heart's connection
to my higher realms
eases discomfort
and my fears of letting go.

I thank you that I may
freely and easily subdue all tension
and unrelenting grasp
of all now and future decisions,
to allow the best coincidences
for all involved.

I thank you that my soul,
spirit and conscious self
are willed to fall freely and unconditionally
into God's sincere and secure palm.

I thank you that every cell
in every dimension
of my body and ego
release all control
to my powerful source.

I thank you that my infinite power of love
allows me to let go
of all binding and forceful actions,
and that I am free from the necessity
to abide by intentions
and decisions of my ego.

I thank you that I easily release
all fear of becoming lost
in the ocean of nothingness.

I am one with God's breath of being.

৩ Seeking Guidance ৩

I thank you that all cause
of perplexity and doubt
are now placed in the hands
of my universal mother.

I thank you that I am free and willing
to align my inner faith and inspiration
with God's spiritual guidance.

I thank you that my fears and joys
are elevated to the consciousness
and power of my true spirit.

I thank you that God's love
expands my soul and mind
with unconditional acceptance,
understanding and creativity,
to guide me to achieving
my perfect goal.

I thank you that my heart is yearning
to fulfill the spirit and wisdom
of my universal plan,
in every aspect
of my dimensional reality.

I am one with every now
in joyous compatibility
with my God presence.

⟡ Achieving Higher Frequency ⟡

I thank you that my cells allow,
accept and assimilate
the continual flow of universal light
in every plane and aspect
of my physical and subtle bodies.

I thank you that my oneness
is continuously established
with my wholeness of spirit and mind,
that my capacity to grow
in frequency is multiplied.

I thank you that the miracle of existence
in light and wisdom
is felt and cherished,
that I am aware of the vibrancy
of potential consciousness.

I thank you for the peaceful
release of structures
that block the flow
of my expanding light and growth.

I thank you for the fine tuning
of all physical, emotional, mental
and spiritual auric fields
in perfect relationship
to my mind and soul.

I thank you that my cells of reality
are attuned to ecstatic frequencies
of God's fulfilling rays of light
to elevate my consciousness
and well-being.

God's light is the air I breathe.

◔ Growing into Divine Connection ◔

I thank you that all restrictions
of my mind, heart and senses
through religious ties,
ceremonies, doctrines,
magnetic frequencies of limitation
and institutions of undermining structures
that bind my senses
is freed and neutralized.

My mind is in peace and in the power of bliss.

I thank you that my mind,
heart and senses
are guided and protected
by my highest being
of universal intelligence,
while holding the frequency
of unwavering devotion
in my highest heart-mind plane,
in the indestructible light of my source.

I thank you for all vibrations
of light and love
that create my well-being,
that awaken my passion
and understanding of ultimate oneness
with my universal family,
my universal ancestors
and my universal self.

I thank my subconscious self,
conscious self, intellect, ego,
higher self, soul, oversoul,
second soul, second oversoul, monad,
spiritual guide, guardian angels,
cosmic helpers, creator,
and universal source
that I now accept and understand
the wonderful, free and ever
manifesting being that I am,
that I now create and embrace
joy and beauty in every region
of my time-space existence.

I thank you that I now let go
of resistance, restriction
and all barriers
of my emotional, illusionary self
that diminish my healing potential
in all facets of my earth existence
and keep me from fully empowering
my divine wholeness,
wellness and healthiness.

I thank you that my clearness of intention
be expressed in my daily being,
in empathy with my heart-soul,
for the elevation of my being
into higher frequencies of matrices.

Mine is the love of peace and pure purpose.

I thank you for the release
from the cycle of inflicted pain,
fear and faithlessness
throughout all time and place,
of my former and future existing planes,
that my being transcends
these limitations in my existence now.

I thank you that my heart is aligned with
focus and intent on pure light
and that these higher heart frequencies
open all doors of patience, tolerance,
acceptance, willingness, calmness,
tranquility, refinement of judgment,
clarity, sovereignty
and choice of light over darkness.

Mine is the unification of light with my highest self.

I thank you for the freedom and power
of living my genuine self
and that my knowingness of oneness
determines the predominant thoughts
and emotions of my daily frequency.

I thank you that every insufficiency,
lack and limitation of heart, soul and mind
is shed within the very core of my being,
on this earth plane
and each realm of existence.

I thank you for clarity and freedom
in every aspect of my being.

I thank you that my need
for control and greed, envy and coveting
are cleansed and dissolved.

Thank you that I am freed
from all barriers of hate and fear.

I thank you that all my
disempowering thoughts
and fears within this day
are realized and resolved.

Thank you that my deepest fears of loss of:
abundance, loving and supporting beings,
self and inner convictions,
rights and reputation,
freedom of choice and speech,
compassion and intensity,
hope and miracles,
light and clarity
are rendered powerless
and fill me with the guidance
and direction of higher purpose
and fulfillment.

I am the everlasting love of universe.

I thank you that I may see
my lack of tolerance, acceptance
and love for myself
and all other existence.

Thank you that I may transcend
my illusions, ego and self-deception.

Thank you for my divine capacity
of perception and cognition.

Thank you for the lightness in my heart,
my burden-free life in all cells of my being
in the reality of my intimate God self.

Thank you that I transform
my fears and doubts
with the power of my knowingness
of universal love.

I thank you for my ultimate position in
God's grace and loving kindness.

I am the spirit and soul of universal light.

I thank you that all disconnections
within my elevating structures of existence
are repaired with universal light
and are healed of self-inflicted pain
and damnation.

Mine is the light that shines in all dimensions of being.

Thank you that I let go
of my personal barriers
in order to house and hold
my highest good of universal essence.

I am connected with the universal light-mind-truth.

I thank you for the miracles of this day,
in this time and space
that cleanse my soul
and allow full focus
on my flawless self,
that all restrictions of illusions
and distortion of reality
are lifted and minimized.

Mine is the love of light
and the light of love
in all facets and dimensions.

Thank you for my willingness
to reach out for, accept and take
my ultimate share of God's miracles.

I am one with my highest
universal mind-consciousness.

⟨ Love of Being ⟩

I thank you for the gift of life,
that I cherish each moment
in harmony and bliss.

I thank you that in every now
my vision reflects God's beauty and grace
in my every feeling,
thought and expression.

I thank you that my joyful being
is expressed in shining light,
that my heart sings
in the warmth of God's loving voice.

I thank you that I fully
recognize and appreciate
the significance of my life
and the precious opportunity
to live, grow and develop my potential.

I thank you that my being is filled
with confidence and encouragement
through God's loving
support and compassion.

I thank you that I embrace
this life on earth
in reverence, esteem and thankfulness,
of prosperity, happiness and love.

✑ Growing in Patience ✑

I thank you that my
continuing perseverance
to develop courage
and toleration
are predominant
in my daily life experience.

I thank you that I am ready
to see the bigger truth
in all events taking place around me,
that I am willing to realize and feel
the rewards bestowed upon me.

I thank you that I
am ready to accept
my position in relation to others
and to my current present self,
that I am aware and willing to allow
the boundaries of my momentary level.

I thank you that universal assistance
supports me to achieve rewarding goals,
divine truth and happiness.

❧ Perseverance of Spiritual Growth ❧

I thank you that God's love
envelops my heart
and fills me with the inspiration
of my true essence.

I thank you for warmth
of spirit, soul and mind
that surrounds my being
in the healing light of grace,
forgiveness and freedom from doubt.

I thank you for the caring support,
embracing and tranquility
of the core of my being
from the highest aspect
of my godliness.

God is my love and power that fills my vessel with joy.

I thank you that my heart is open
to the expression of joy,
balance and integrity.

God is my certainty of happiness.

I thank you for the safety
of the protection, the unwavering light,
the sovereignty and the certainty
of God's infinite power.

I thank you that I
am now willed to surrender
to God's loving support.

ᕫ Increasing Soul Energy ᕫ

I thank you that all
my significant feelings
of love and openness
are fulfilled and sacred
in my heart of sentient being.

I thank you that my heart-soul structures
are polished and formed
in the ultimate sense
of my soul's plan and passion.

I thank you that my heart-soul-spirit
is in harmony with everlasting peace.

I thank you that I am able and willing
to open all doors
in my heart's inner chambers
to allow the full capacity
of my soul energy to reside.

I thank you that my heart is ready
to embrace and understand every facet
of my divine soul spirit,
which flow freely
in my daily thoughts and feelings.

I thank you that I may
unconditionally fulfill
the utmost purpose
of my highest soul-self.

I thank you for the ultimate connection
between the earth-crystal,
my heart- and soul-crystal,
and the centre of my position
in God's universe.

I thank you that my crystal being
of enduring light form,
is the radiant being of oneness
with my heart-crystal.

My heart, soul and mind are the
everlasting light of God.

I thank you that all blockages
that undermine my well-being
and allowance of fulfillment
are released.

I thank you that all chambers of my heart
are connected to form one vast chamber
of highest regard and intense love
for all existence, matter and energy.

I am God's love of soul and spirit.

The
Physical Body

The Physical Body

Before working in the physical body ALL blockages have to be removed. Otherwise it is almost impossible to be satisfied with the results. The blockages build a resistance that prevents the healing effect.

In fact, miracles do not exist. They sometimes seem to exist, providing that the preliminary work has been done. Healing techniques all over the world have one very important factor in common. If the patient or client has 'understood' the reason and integrated the necessary change, that person is ready to be healed.

What makes it complicated is that you often don't remember when the origin of the problem took place. The cause of the dysfunction happened in former lives, in other planes of existence, etc. If someone is claustrophobic, for instance, and has never had a bad experience such as being captured or burned in a confined place ... the cause is most likely in the past, where a similar dramatic event took place. Our subtle bodies store all of our experiences, in every existence, in every time and place. You will be reminded of the original experience and react fearfully. This is a self-protection mechanism, that is very likely outdated.

Unfortunately, what separates people from miraculous healings are the many hidden blockages, and fears, they have not yet resolved. Anything can be manifested if there are no obstacles.

You may ask if fears are helpful and necessary to protect yourself at all times. However, you can only protect yourself if you react correctly in the given situation. Fear prevents you from staying calm and evaluating the danger. It is the elimination or neutralization of fear that helps you to connect to your highest self for the appropriate answers you need to intuitively prevent danger.

When working on the physical body, address the prayers to your body's consciousness as well. That way your body will not resist the changes.

❧ Protection from Radioactivity ❧

I thank you for the perfect alignment
in all centers of my being
and the connection of all cells,
bodies and systems.

I thank you for the activation and balance
of all spiral energy forms
and pulsating light frequencies
that fill each and every existing cell
with the natural protection
of God's grace and compassion.

I thank you that the continuous
flow of divine light
resists any harm and destruction
from radioactive informational frequencies.

I thank you for the perpetual renewal
and liberation of my physical body
from all lethal matter
and radioactive residue
in every time, space and dimension.

My body is God's temple of spirit.

✤ Reducing Pain ✤

I thank you that all frequencies of fear,
resistance and lack of trust
held within my cells of existence
that connect my being with physical pain,
emotional sorrow and resignation,
are released and freed.

I thank you that my unfulfilled
yearning is resolved.

Mine is the glory and joy of my physical manifestation.

I thank you that I now let go
of all anxiety and stress
that blocks my flow
of ease and well-being.

I thank you that all
structures of dependence
that undermine my confidence
and joy of decision
are filled with light and love.

❧ Supporting Good Health ❧

I thank you that God's
universal healing power
heals and harmonizes me
with the frequency of love
and forgiveness.

I thank you for the miracle of oneness
of my body and soul with divine grace,
that I may recognize and understand
my personal patterns
of dysfunction and disease.

I thank you for the deepest
warmth and undivided love
for my physical body.

I thank you that my kidneys,
my liver and my spleen
are connected with the everlasting
breath of God,
filling my matrices
with continuous soul information
and optimal earth energy.

I thank you that all my body's parts and functions
are flawlessly coordinated
in every dimension of my being.

I thank you that God is one
with my spirit and the resolution
of perfect health and vitality,
that my youthful strength
is restored and revived
in all my thoughts, feelings
and physical body.

I thank you that my purpose
is elevated and unified
with all my planes of existence,
that withhold my highest
health and wellbeing
to the fullest consciousness
of my soul, body and mind.

❧ The Miracle of the Physical Body ❧

I thank you that every cell,
facet and fathom
of my physical body is now
in perfect health, youth,
polarity and harmony.

I thank you that programs of damage
and aging in all my cells
are released and nullified
in all dimensional planes of my body.

I thank you that every tissue,
cell and system
is coordinated, aligned and synchronized
with the every now planet constellation,
asset of peace, well-being,
perfect balance and cell restoration.

I thank you that my mind
is one with the flow
of God's wonder and harmony,
that all my matrices are replenished
and restored in God's perfect image.

I thank you that all my glands
are in connection and communication
with God's fine clockwork
of body functions,
and are readjusted
to the perfect flow
of God's replenishing impulse
in every physical cell.

I thank you that all synapses
in my mind system
are renewed, restored and connected
that allow me to receive God's
miracles, love and ecstasy.

I thank you that all my organs,
bones, muscles ...
are in harmony with each other
and working together
for freedom from pain,
illness and discordant energy,
in each and every atom of my body.

I am God's perfect image of body, soul and mind.

I am one with God's replenishment
of life and cosmic balance.

I am one with God's grace and fulfillment
in every atom of my breath.

I thank you, for the perfect coordination
of body, mind and soul
with God's everlasting healing light
of constant replenishment,
restoration and oneness.

I thank you that all human cells
are washed from distortion,
dysfunction and pain
in every infinite moment
of my physical reality.

I thank you that all matrices of sickness,
ill health and weakness
are disconnected and void of validity
in all dimensions, time and space.

I thank you that all shocks
of pain and violence
are lifted and dispersed
and that my physical body
is free of every memory of pain.

I am one with God's perfect image
of health, youth and beauty.

❧ Improving Eyesight ❧

I thank you that I may see clear and free
through my eyes of abundance.

I thank you that my heart is willing
to receive all truth in relation to reality
in all facets of my being.

Thank you that I see the perfection of this universe.

I thank you that my eyes
are now in perfect coherence
with my life task
of cherishing and embracing
the gift of life.

I thank you for my willingness to see
and respect God's judgment,
faith and grace.

I am the loving consequence of God's guiding light.

I thank you that all distortion
that may arise
from fear of seeing
and accepting reality
of the third dimension
be diminished and discredited.

I am embedded in God's heaven on earth.

I thank you for
the perfect condition of my eyes
and the surrounding systems of my eyes
for my perfect eyesight,
unclogged of any disturbing
strain and residue,
due to self-imposed feelings
of guilt and condemnation
for the suffering
of my parents and ancestors.

I thank you for the harmonic
coherence and coordination
of all my mucous membrane
with all systems of moisture
and with the perfect balance
of all fluid and hormone systems,
that relieve all dryness.

My body is God's balance of love and
harmony, self-forgiveness and faith.

God is my wisdom and strength.

I thank you that I am ready
to release all self-imposed torment,
that my being is protected
from all frequencies of hate, greed
and the loss of hope.

God's support and freedom of judgment
are my optimal eyesight.

I thank you that all coagulated, harmful,
irritating, foreign substance and matter
are cleansed and illuminated
from the power of my being,
from my tissues
and from the delicate functions
of my body's systems.

I thank you for the continuous
flow and balance
of my hormonal system, that replenish
and restore every cell with elasticity
and regeneration in every now moment.

I thank you that every stress, strain
and blurriness in my eyes
is calmed and cleansed
in order to allow and support
my perfect sight in every now.

I thank you that my eyesight
is free from distortion and weakness
in any given situation.

I thank you that I am willing
to see and forgive
my flaws and imperfections,
to stop all self-judgment
and to allow self-recognition.

I am the fulfilled eyes of God.

❧ Repairing Synapses ❧

I thank you that all synapses in my brain
are freed from unforgiveness,
emotional pain and destruction.

I thank you that all connecting strands
are repaired, healed and filled with light.

I thank you that all doorways
to my heart of comfort and compassion
are opened and secured
with joyful and everlasting peace.

I thank you that fear and self-pity
are cured and genuinely shed,
and that my inner child
is in balance with my soul's just cause.

I am the enduring light and faith of the divine source.

❦ Balancing Hormones ❦

I thank you that the wonderful creation
of my youthful body is regenerated
and renewed in every moment of now.

I thank you that my cells
in all my systems and bodies
are purified and cleansed
from toxic waste,
degeneration and decay.

I thank you that my body
and all my vital organs
are nourished from the God mother
of beauty, ecstasy and fulfillment.

I thank you that my body
is young and replenished
in every reality, time
and space of my existence
and therefore the perfect temple
for the miracle of my soul.

I thank you that my vibrant
and expanding being
and all my body's functions,
glands and organs
regenerate and multiply my vitality
in a permanent, constant
and automatic fashion.

God mother is my everlasting
source of youth and agility.

❧ Balancing Frequency ❧

I thank you that all frequencies
in my third dimensional planes of existence
are coordinated and harmonized
with my heart, my cells and my being.

I thank you that all systems
are aligned and opened
to the ultimate flow of energy
and the power of God's stability.

I thank you for the perfect supplement
of connecting strands in my matrix
of physical, emotional
and mental well-being.

❧ Staying Young ❧

I thank you physical body and soul
for sustaining my perfect youth.

I thank now all my cells, my organs,
my glands, my muscles, my bones,
my veins and my body tissues
for repeatedly and consistently
regenerating in the perfect fashion
of youthful, self-perpetuating renewal.

I thank you for the wondrous rejuvenation
of my physical body in this now moment.

I thank you for the correspondence
of all my bodily frequencies
in coordination with my higher bodies,
in accordance with my soul body.

I thank you that all processes
of my physical body
consistently induce and support
the perfect removal
of all toxins and wastes
in the quickest possible manner,
that otherwise would have
a degenerating effect on my tissues.

I am the everlasting youthfulness
and agility of physical body.

❧ Releasing Toxins ❧

I thank you that all my body's functions,
digestion, respiration and heart circulation
are attuned and coordinated
in frequency and balance
with the ultimate concept of God's image.

I thank you that my body's consciousness
is willing to allow and support
the perfect performance
of each cell in perfect relationship
to each other and in accordance
with my highest goal of infinity, immortality,
regeneration and ascension.

I thank you that all toxins are released
in proportion and relation
to the acceptance and allowance
of my physical consciousness
in the now moment
in accordance to sustained vitality.

I thank you that my excretory organs
are free, resilient and fit
for perfect
regeneration and functionality.

I thank you that my emotional body
is ready to release
all handicaps, barriers and resistance
that might harm or incapacitate
my microstructures.

I thank you that my body is free
from all impurities now.

My body is the perfect example of God's temple.

❧ Losing Weight ❧

I thank you that all cravings
of my physical body
that seek fulfillment
through indulgent consumption of food
are curbed and limited,
in order to allow losing all overweight.

I thank you that my body
is willing to let go
of all extra pounds
and nonetheless enjoy eating
the version of nutrition
that achieves my goals of staying young,
sporty and slender.

I thank you that my appetite is fitted
to the perfect molding of my physical form
in the expression of my true
original youth and beauty.

The Physical Body

I thank you that all physical discomfort
during losing weight be reduced
and all letting go of waste particles
take place without causing pain
or harm for the physical body.

I thank you for my perfect metabolism,
which allows me to digest
every eaten food quickly and properly,
so that I stay fit and slender
in every situation.

I thank you that my digestion
is coordinated
with my physical
and emotional frequencies,
and that my appetite
is always fulfilled and satisfied.

I thank you for my yearning and joy
of physical exercise that atones
and shapes my figure
into a beautiful mould
of dainty curves
or perfect muscles.

I thank you that every breath I take
reduces that overabundance
of fat and toxins,
that keep me from achieving
my perfect and slender
dress size or suite size of ??
and weight of ?? pounds.

I thank you that my physical appearance
is the perfect reflection
of my inner aesthetic, slender
and feminine or masculine figure,
which I am able to image
in every now moment.

I know now that I am always young, thin, and agile.

I am the reflection, charm and beauty of God's grace.

Thank you, thank you, thank you.

❧ Expanding Brain Capacity ❧

I thank you that all segments of my brain
are attuned and unified
with my universal mind.

I thank you that the connections
that are severed are now linked,
cleared and willing
to receive universal,
expanding knowledge.

I thank you that my mind
and clarity of spirit
are rejoined and prepared
to perpetuate in amplitude
of universal knowledge and high frequency.

I thank you that my heart
and mind are one
to bring forth the eternal
and ever growing source of wisdom
and divine information.

I thank you for the flow
of increasing energy
through me and within me
that enhance and consequentially open
every facet of my mind
to its fullest potential of knowledge.

I thank you that I am in memory
of my existing time and space
to access the answers to my questions,
containing universal law,
past, present and future.

I thank you for my oneness
and my wholeness
of body, soul and spirit
that nurture my thought patterns
with divine truth.

I am the ever expanding experience
of universal knowledge.

The
Emotional
Body

The Emotional Body

You have the power to love unconditionally. To love unconditionally is to be unconditional. It means to accept yourself and others just as they are. Your experiences of fear and injustice have separated you from others. You have created barriers to protect yourself. Unfortunately, they have the opposite effect. They protect you from being loved.

To receive love, you have to open your heart and let go of all grudges and illusions of being the victim. Only an open heart can protect you. To open your heart, all pain and suffering must be dissolved and healed.

The following prayers will help you to do so. You can repeat them as often as you feel that they will purify you and allow the mending and healing process. If you enjoy and savour each word, they will elevate you and raise your frequency.

✍ Healing the Heart ✍

I thank you that all facets of my heart
are purified and whole
in the perfection of my soul-heart-crystal.

I thank you that all heart matrices
are aligned and attuned
to my divine axis and flow
in unity with my light essence.

I thank you that all incidents
that are responsible
for my distorted and interrupted
connections to my godly existence,
are peacefully joined
and that all shared abundance
is restored in God's faith and trust.

I thank you that my heart is radiant
with the light of my being
from the highest
of my soul's evolving spheres.

I thank you that the capacity and potential
of my heart's loving spirit
fills and fulfills my entire planetary being
in this existing plane.

🌿　🌿　🌿

✍ Opening the Heart ✍

I thank you that my trusting heart
is forever embedded in lasting peace
and divine ecstasy.

I thank you that all facets of my heart
shine clear, strong and in harmony.

I thank you that my heart matrices
are free from all wounds, disappointment
and disempowering experiences.

I thank you that my heart is synchronized
and vastly connected
with my eternal godlike being.

I thank you that my heart
is open at all times
to the guidance of and oneness with
God's loving care.

I am the expression of universal love.

✑ Strengthening the Heart ✑

I thank you that all
my structures are alligned,
defined and coordinated,
to reach the perfect balance
of heart and soul.

I thank you that I am clear
and open to love, light and ecstasy
in all structures of my heart,
free of judgment and fear.

I thank you that my heart's aspects
are in accordance with God's will
and everlasting peace, joy
and unconditional love.

I thank you that all discordant energy in
my past, present and future
is forgiven and neutralized
through God's grace and light.

I am the frequency of God's loving and giving heart.

✐ Connecting the Heart ✐

I thank you for the continuous expansion
of connecting pathways
that allow my heart energy to reach and elevate
each and every chakra, meridian
and all other subtle structures.

I thank you that my
organs, tissues, cells,
and all other physical structures
are now synchronized with the frequency
of my pure heart.

I thank you that my breath
and heart work together
to spread my heart's qualities
of compassion, understanding, loving joy
generosity, acceptance, tolerance,
worthiness, appreciation,
and all other attributes of love.

I thank you that my heart and mind
work together for the ultimate goal
of my godlike self
to live and to be
that which I truly am,
free of all constrictions
and self-inflicted restrictions.

I thank you that
the thankfulness in my heart
touches and fathoms every layer of my cells
and fills my being with infinite wealth
in all facets of my thankful being.

I am God's love of living, being and existing.

⟋ Feeling Wanted ⟋

I thank you that my deepest fear
of being abandoned or replaced
is neutralized and healed
to gain serenity
and tender comfort in my daily
thoughts, feelings and convictions.

I thank you that I am in peaceful
and happy relations
with myself, with God
and all living beings around me.

I thank you that I
am guided and supported
in every living moment
to co-exist and to find my rightful,
safe and secure place
among society, friends, parents, family,
authorities, teachers
and all other living beings
that surround me.

God is my inner balance and sense of belonging.

I thank you that I may daily feel,
realize and understand
the gift of God's endless friendship and care
in every facet of life.

I thank you that I am filled
with courage and trust
in myself, my life upon this earth planet
and this universe.

God's trust and faith make me free.

✍   ✍   ✍

✍ Feeling Loved and Cherished ✍

I thank you that my soul and being
are connected and unified
with all my dimensions of existence,
with my self and all aspects of consciousness.

I thank you that I feel the infallible bond,
the unique flowing rays
of God's loving and cherishing commitment.

I thank you that my being
is connected in continuous harmony
with my soul family, my brothers and sisters,
through the shining light of fortitude and compassion.

I thank you that my days on earth are distinguished
through the infinite and uplifting power
of the highest God presence,
in all times of doubts, needs and longings.

I thank you that my mind and my focus of reality
are forever inspired with the abundance of love,
through universal heart, mind and spirit.

✍ ✍ ✍

℘ Feeling Special ℘

I thank you that my oneness with God's spirit
allows me to see myself
in my true and perfect light.

I thank you that I am aware of the uniqueness
of my being, my spirit and soul
in the wholeness of God's existence.

I thank you for my unfalsified insight
into others, their origin, their spirit and soul,
and my oneness with all existing beings.

I thank you for the recognition
of my very special role
among God's creation
of all living beings,
within my intimate connection
to all that is.

℘   ℘   ℘

☞ Feeling Worthy of Love ☜

I thank you that I am open and willing
to accept love in all cells of my being.

I thank you that denial of love
in all facets of my existence
is dissolved, dispersed and healed.

I thank you that my soul and mind
and all facets of my dimensions
are fulfilled with endless rays
of illuminating love essence,
that shine and fill me
with God's wonder of love.

I thank you for the unity of spirit,
soul and mind
in my vast potential of shining grace.

I thank you that my heart
is soothed of all pain
and endurance of failure,
suffering and stress
that I have inflicted upon myself,
that have cut me off from the worthiness
of universal love.

I thank you that all chambers of my heart
are willing to accept and utilize
the flow of God's light energy,
submitting all gaps and tears
to the oneness of God's harmony.

I thank you that the radiance
of love's healing grace
allows a new beginning
of trusting and feeling
the strength of my heart capacity.

I am one with the healing grace of universal love.

✐ Releasing Anger ✐

I thank you that my heart,
mind and soul
are relieved and cleansed
of angering thoughts and emotions.

I thank you that I am aware
of personal weakness
in every seemingly unjust situation
and incomplete information
leading to blind convictions
in my every moment of expressing anger.

I thank you that my mind
is now in balance
with my capacity
of understanding and compassion
and that all my actions and reactions
in my daily thoughts are evident,
in accordance and conclusive.

I thank you that I
am willing to accept without regret
my 'wrong' doings
and I am able to transform them
with the consequence
of perfect responsibility
into the pure frequency of forgiveness.

I thank you that my higher knowledge
of God's just universe
penetrates my every cell
and fills me with peace and confidence.

I am free of anger and the frequencies
of fear and injustice.

✑ Releasing Resentment ✑

I thank you that I am willing
to see the broader picture,
all the pieces and all information
withheld from my ego,
that help me understand and resolve
the core of my resentment.

I thank you that my heart is free
to join in harmony with all people,
places and incidents involved
that distort my feelings, thoughts and insight
and detach me from my
truth and understanding.

I thank you that my soul and my ego
are cleansed of all bruises and pains
that disfigure and dispute
my connection with God's higher intent.

I thank you that
my empathy and compassion
connect me with all existing beings
as I comprehend the deepest abyss
of fears and pains
shared by all.

ᗜ **Releasing Regret** ᗜ

I thank you that I am relieved
of all self-blame and regrets from my past, present and future.

I thank you that all negative experiences,
due to poor judgment and false decisions
are released, through
my growing awareness
that I have thereafter achieved.

I thank you for the balance in my timeline
of regret and discontent
that have led me
and my unconscious being
to the void of self-reproach.

I thank you that I am cleansed

of every painful reflection
which has cost
my confidence and enthusiasm.

I thank you that my past is released
and that I am filled
with the wisdom of experience,
the glory of the present
and the joy of the future.

✍ Reducing Worry and Emotional Pain ✍

I thank you that all burdens, stress,
worries, anxiety and self-blame
misery and pain,
disgrace, unworthiness,
downfalls and failure
are now and forever neutralized.

I thank you that my soul
may rejoice anew every day
in deep inner peace and content.

I thank you that my loving spirit guides
show me the light and joy,
the freedom in every minute of my day
that I would otherwise forfeit.

I thank you that every dream,
reality and chain reaction
is held in the frequency of light,
bliss and loving inspiration,
that free me of illusions
and negative belief patterns
reflecting despair, doubt and distrust.

I am free to be
secure and safe,
truthful and responsible,
thankful and faithful,
consequent and persistent,
worthy and capable of
creativity and self-expression,
optimism and happiness,
maturity and wisdom,
patience and insight,
liberation from dependency,
composure and reflection,
trust and confidence,
achievement and success.

Thank you that it is so now.

✐ Self-Acceptance ✐

I thank you that all
my failures and imperfections
are dissolved and healed
in the vastness of God's loving presence
in every cell and every dimension
of my universal essence.

I thank you that I am unified with
my conscious loving highest self and shining light
and that I now experience myself
in every facet of my godlike qualities.

I thank you that I realize
that the spirit presence within me
makes me perfect and whole,
a mirror to God's image, in every aspect.

I thank you that my thankful heart
expresses the ecstasy of universal love
and joy of my existence.

✐　✐　✐

✍ Feeling Beautiful ✍

I thank you that the reality
of my physical body
is touched by God's love and grace.

I thank you that the loveliness
of my soul and mind
shine and glow in my physical cells,
that my highest being and unique qualities
are seen and recognized.

I thank you that my heart and body are joined
with my true and universal spirit,
and my personal expression of pleasure,
satisfaction and charm.

I thank you that my conscious mind
is willing to feel, see, hear,
touch and taste
the perfect beauty
in every now existence
in my every now being.

✍ ✍ ✍

✍ Eliminating Self-Pity ✍

I thank you that my honest intention
to grow spiritually
leads me to realize
and understand all patterns
of self-pity.

Thank you that I am aware
of all action and reaction
that I have put in motion,
that lead to dissatisfaction
and discontent.

Thank you that I am able to feel
the fullest confidence in my ability
to learn and grow.

Thank you that I am ready
to see all cause and effect
in accordance to life and reality,
therefore able to live
in peaceful joy.

I thank you that I am the frequency
of responsibility of my actions
and freedom of choice
to release all self-pity.

I am universal freedom of spirit.

✐ Reducing Self-Doubt ✐

I thank you that all thoughts
of disappointment, doubt and resignation
are dissolved and released.

I thank you that my lightness of heart,
trust and confidence rapidly grow
to enhance my highest spirit
and bring forth
my inner strength and vision.

I thank you that I am ready and willing
to know and feel the compassion
of my inner God presence
throughout every cell of my being,
and the certainty of who I am.

I thank you that my trust is restored,
encouraged through confidence
in my self and my actions.

I am the reflection of God's courage,
faith and fulfillment.

✐   ✐   ✐

✑ Feeling Hope ✑

I thank you that my hope
and assurance are restored,
as failure and despair give way.

I thank you that all disappointment
and disempowerment are dissolved,
and that I am open to begin again
in my new path of thankfulness.

I thank you that I am fully convinced
that all events, no matter
how they might appear,
are for my best
and most important experience,
in God's framework
of growing fulfillment.

I thank you that all barriers are overcome
for the quest of my soul and spirit,
to rise above all hopelessness and fear.

I thank you that I am able to see and feel
the light in every darkness
and the support of God in every defeat.

I am God's clarity, vision and magnitude of hope.

✍ Respect ✍

I thank you God
that I feel, see and hear
the complexity and wonder
of the earth's vision of existence.

I thank you that I
realize and appreciate
the complexity and multitude
of each and every living being
in the earth's entirety of existence.

I thank you that my understanding and empathy
of God's greater ambition and cause
to unite all beings in respect and equality
helps me respect and be respected
as a valuable member of God's kingdom.

I am embedded in the source of I am.

✍ Feeling Calm ✍

I thank you that all tension
is dissolved and released
through the lightness
of my knowing spirit and mind.

I thank you that all structures
of unworthiness or sightlessness are deleted
and that I am in my inner calm,
where all solutions are evident and clear.

I am one with my flow of spirit and soul,
in balance with the universe.

I am protected and stable
in the chambers of my heart,
where I breathe the atmosphere
of peace and tranquility.

I thank you for my heart's shining grace
in every cell of my emotional
and mental bodies.

I thank you that all thought patterns of distress
are quiet and distant,
and that I am one with the natural flow
of universal breath.

I am one with peace.

✑ Feeling and Being Safe ✑

I thank you that my infinite trust and faith
in the caring and loving God,
are restored and healed.

I thank you that my tarnished vision,
caused by fear and anger
is washed and balanced
through the knowledge and grace
of God's truth in every past and present
facet of existence.

I thank you that I am held and protected
in all moments of doubt and despair
and the reality of my deepest beliefs
of evil, injustice and punishment
are released and give way
to the power and strength
of my true conviction of love,
justice and peace.

I thank you for my awareness at all times
of God's safety and protection
in every moment and every cell of my being.

✑   ✑   ✑

✍ Preventing Mobbing ✍

I am one with all that is light
and love in this universe,
my creator and all my supporting beings
in the twelfth plane of existence.

I thank you for your wonderful guidance,
full of clarity and inspiration
that sever and heal all my ties
with beings using and profiting
from my energy field.

I bless them and let them free for other experiences.

I thank you for the limitation
they have enabled me to feel
and therefore to grow
in conviction and strength.

✍ ✍ ✍

✐ Partnership ✐

I thank you that all vibrations
of receiving, giving and accepting
that are projected from my heart,
soul and mind,
are answered and fulfilled
with everlasting loving partnership.

I thank you that I am appreciated,
understood, supported and embraced
in all parts of my being
and bestowed with my perfect match
in this now.

I thank you that I am willing to let go
of all barriers of hurt, fear and sadness
that separate me from passion,
desire and ecstasy.

I am God's grace and intensity of fulfillment.

I thank you that all feminine/masculine
qualities of my heart are elevated
strengthened and balanced
to a higher frequency
of magnificent glory and wonder.

I thank you that every broken heart
be mended and healed
so that I may achieve full capacity
of fulfilling and unconditional love.

I am the love of God's heart.

ᕲ Balancing Gender ᕲ

I thank you that my heart
is in perfect balance
of passive and active forces.

I thank you that my right to be
is acclaimed and settled
and that I may live at ease.

I thank you that my warmth and strength
are intertwined in deep harmony,
that I may live
the quality of my perfect polarity.

I thank you that my inner feelings
and point of view are in alliance
with my male/female counterpart,
with whom I am whole in my soul.

I thank you that my body structures are matched
with the feminine/masculine expression
that is fitting to this inner conviction.

I thank you that my being reflects
the epitome of power and grace.

I am God's completeness of male and female aspects.

Letting Go of Fear

I thank you that I let go now
of all drama that controls me
and blocks me from living the vastness
and safety of my fearless self.

I thank you that I am void
of envy, jealousy, resentment,
regret, shame, anxiety,
distress, expectation, vulnerability,
control, inferiority and blame
that keep me bound
to my primitive survival instincts.

I thank you that I am full of confidence
in myself, the universe,
my friends and family,
that I know the best
and most wonderful solution
will appear at the right time.

I thank you that I live each day
in positive conviction,
that every possible fear
is dissipated and lost
to my endless, limitless faith.

❧   ❧   ❧

✐ Maintaining Concentration ✐

I thank you that the
hemispheres of my brain
are united and coordinated.

I thank you that all
aspects of my brain
are balanced and activated,
for the purpose
of perfect concentration.

I thank you that all alignment
is consequentially achieved,
that connect my heart,
my soul and my brain
to the wholeness of my mind.

I thank you that all structures of diversion
are dissolved and annulled,
to allow the creativity
of my mind's true thoughts and insights.

I thank you that I am one
with the subject of my concentration
in this very moment
and every further moment aspired.

I am one with my mind's full capacity and potential.

Thank you.

🖎 🖎 🖎

✆ Stability and Steadiness ✆

I thank you that my heart, mind and soul
are aware and knowing
of the correlations and connections,
of the path I have chosen.

I thank you that I am centered and focused
in all situations of emotional instability,
fear and anguish
that predominate in my heart, body and soul
and disperse my energy
from my higher goals and aims.

I thank you that my perspective
is high and clear
and that I know and feel
at any given moment
my perfect position
in God's reality.

I thank you that I am the eyes, ears and breath
of God's wisdom in all time and space.

✍ Fulfillment ✍

I thank you for my merits,
strengths, talents and inner wealth
to which I now have access,
which I now integrate
to the fullest capacity of my being.

I thank you that my life is blessed
with my profound ability and longing
to express my highest divine potential
in the highest good
of my soul and spirit.

I thank you that I live now
the wondrous diversity and challenge
that enhance and support
my inherent divine spark
and reward my cause
with satisfaction and delight.

I thank you that my blissful light
that I shine and reflect
shows others the path
to pleasure and happiness.

✍   ✍   ✍

✍ Happiness ✍

I thank you that all destructive emotions
that block my view and tarnish my aura
are cleared, and that my being is free
to express gratitude, happiness and bliss.

I thank you that I am aware and thankful
for my courage and determination
to understand and grasp,
with God's presence and support,
the true meaning of my daily challenges.

I thank you that I am enlightened
with joy and happiness,
inner wisdom and faith
that show me each blessing
despite each barrier, burden and fear
in every seemingly hopeless situation.

I thank you that I am able
to comprehend and appreciate
the chance in every complexity
the strength in every weakness
the joy in every sadness
and the gift of happiness.

✍ ✍ ✍

The Challenge
of
Daily Living

✑ Finding Solutions ✑

I thank you that I am willing
to see beyond the burden
of diverting choice
far from distraction
and illusion.

I thank you that my mind
and heart are one
to formulate the perfect question
that I may fathom the full capacity
of the problem at hand.

I thank you that my heart and head
are open to new ways and answers
in the vast creativity
of God's universal infinity.

I thank you that I realize and adapt
to the endless support and inspiration
of universal mind power.

I thank you that my faith and trust
in God's ability and power
flow through me
to manifest through me
a multitude of happiness and fulfillment
void of limitation.

I thank you for my perfect
sensibility and understanding
of the universal language
to guide me through all situations
into ideal solutions
for each and every being involved.

I thank you for the flawless vision
in moments of solitude
that helps me see the best reality
in the best setting, time and place.

God's support, guidance and grace are mine
in every dimension of my being.

∽ Stress ∽

I thank you that all weight of stress,
worries, defeat and self-judgement,
disgrace, unworthiness and failure
are eased and lifted.

I thank you that my soul can rejoice,
every day anew
in deep inner peace and content.

I thank you that my loving spirit guides
show me the light, joy and freedom
in every minute of my day,
that I would otherwise forfeit.

I thank you that I am held every night
in the frequency of light, joy
and loving inspiration
that free me of all illusions
and negative beliefs.

I thank you that I am free to be worthy
of daily wonders and uplifting experiences
of expanding love in all that I see,
speak, hear, feel and sense.

I thank you that I am free to see
and accept all the gifts life offers me,
the trust and love
of wonderful beings around me.

I thank you that I live and give
the gifts that I am,
in my actions and reactions,
my thoughts and words,
in my strong connection
to the earth's realms of liberty.

I thank you that I am in
the constant frequency of focus
of the beauty, grace
and perfection of my world.

I thank you that God's smile
is within me, upon me
and all around me.

✍ Persistency ✍

I thank you for my willpower
to represent and promote
the just and worthy cause
in accordance with universal plan.

I thank you that I am clear
in my determination and attempt
to be confident and constructive
and to achieve my valuable
and honorable goal.

I thank you that my optimism,
strength and encouragement
radiate and expand
to bring assurance and support
for all involved.

I thank you for my stamina and patience
to hearten and elevate
through persistency and skill
in all divine aspirations, dreams and hopes.

Thank you.

✍   ✍   ✍

✐ Balance of All Realms ✐

I thank you for my conscious effort
to combine, contain and regulate
all dimensions of my existence.

I thank you that all realms of glory
on earth and heaven
are balanced and coordinated
in all my living experiences.

I thank you that all my energy flow
is the perfect combination
of stability, love and godliness.

I thank you for my capacity
to see, trust and embrace
all dimensions of complexity
in its perfect balance.

I am the connecting vision of God's realms.

❧ Job and Creativity ❧

I thank you for the strength,
intelligence and determination
that I feel within myself
to live in fullness of my creativity,
success and prosperity.

I thank you for my acceptance
of all universal gifts
that support my independence,
diligence and willingness
to make my earth life
harmonious and flourishing.

I thank you for my awareness,
stability, and inner peace
that guide me lovingly and effortlessly
to oneness with my god self.

❧ Vocation ❧

I thank you for the perfect opportunity,
time and space
to embrace my soul essence
in every I am.

I thank you for the inspiration
of my highest light
and appreciation of universe
to find my self and my worthy spirit
in my daily life now.

I thank you for the connection
of all neural pathways
that are required now
between my personality,
heart and soul guide
that help me see, feel and realize
my very special
and unique purpose of being.

I thank you for my every moment
of courage, faith and trust
that allow me to shed my fears
to live the purest duty of my essence.

I thank you that I am willing to grasp
and persistently carry through
my chosen goals
to know and live
every highest perspective
that unites me with my inner truth.

I thank you that I am clear and free
of all distracting thoughts, feelings
and activities that bind me
to the unconscious repetition
of false hopes, paths and realities.

I thank you that I am resistant
and unyielding
to the magnetic pull of illusion,
comfort and non-commitment,
that hold me back and keep me
from the expression
and highest potential of my divinity.

I am the creative, expanding purpose of spirit.

∽ Prosperity ∽

I thank you for all gifts,
abundance and inner wealth
that reflect me, surround me
and support me in my highest
and worthiest godlike self.

I thank you that my heritage
and devotion to my divine hierarchy,
to all beings of kindness and compassion
are blessed and reinforced.

I thank you that I am able and willing
to allow my inner richness
and infallible innate creativity
that I now unfold and express.

I thank you for the richness
and magnitude of expansion
in abundance and generosity
of God's infinite flow of prosperity
within me, reflecting me
and manifesting in me and for me.

ᕮ Success ᕮ

I thank you that my awareness and perception
are coordinated with all opportunities
and my heart's endeavors,
coupled with my soul's higher good.

I thank you that my clear and embracing unified heart
is extended, balanced and unified,
that my knowledge and intuition
are sufficiently combined and applied.

I am the faith of God's work and
perfect synchronization.

I thank you for the keys to success
and focus of expansion.

I thank you for the perfect vibration

of wholeness and beingness
in my actions and words and
the wholeheartedness behind
each action and word.

I thank you for the right I have earned
to live my strength and potential
in all dimensions of my vocation.

I am God's perfect example
of success and prosperity.

✑ Supporting Projects ✑

I thank you that I find
confidence in myself,
my skills and my abilities
to hold and guide this project.

I thank you that I progress consistently,
void of despair and doubt,
and that my project arises
with ease and stability.

I thank you that I clearly see, hear
and feel my calling
and receive abundant information
to produce and cultivate
quality and excellence
for all who are involved.

I thank you for this gift
of fulfilling achievement
and the continuance to live
a happy and prosperous life
while serving universal source.

I am my soul's voice and spirit.

Thank you.

◌ Communication ◌

I thank you that my words and feelings
are joined and coordinated
to express my truthful reality.

I thank you that my heart chakra
is connected to all my chakras
and holds me in the frequency
of God's loving inspiration.

I thank you that I am guided
and willed to hear my inner voice
that keeps me attuned
to the perfect communication
in genuine consideration and harmony.

I thank you that my mind's objective
to develop a compassionate
and joyful understanding
is rewarded with completion.

I thank you that my good intentions
form the basis of interaction with others
free of conflict and judgment.

☙ Being Heard ☙

I thank you that my feelings
and thoughts are regarded
with respect and consideration.

I thank you that my opinions
are equal and worthy,
and will be patiently heard
without accusation and ridicule.

I thank you that the complex structures
in the essence of my being
and the expression and manifestation
of my true godlike potential
will be clearly understood.

Thank you.

✑ Friendship ✑

I thank you for the spark
of light that we hold,
that is between us
in all experiences and memories.

I thank you that you are always present,
that we support each other
in the most taxing times.

I thank you that our friendship
is a warm blanket
in all times of stress and sadness.

I thank you that we share
the beauty and harmony of friendship,
understanding and caring,
and our endeavor to trust
and cherish one another.

I thank you for this very special love
that can only be among friends,
two connecting hearts and souls,
in laughter and joy.

I thank you that our friendship is always pure,
void of competition and jealousy,
ready to grow,
to accommodate each change
among each individual.

I thank you for the flexibility and care,
the self-reflection and honesty
that make us free
to be ourselves, regardless of hardship.

☙ Family ☙

I thank you earth, all living beings
and members of my family
that support me and my vision
to learn my essential truth
and to develop and grow
my highest capacity.

I thank you for my family
of soul brothers and sisters,
my spirit guides and guardian angels
that fill my life with fulfillment,
peace and sense of belonging.

I thank you for
my God mother, God father
and the eternal universe
who nurture me, sustain me
and embrace me with loving care
in every facet of my essence.

I thank you that I am never forsaken,
and that I am always embedded
in God's loving heart.

Disconnecting
Dark Entities

Disconnecting
Dark Entities

What meaning does the new era have for each individual? How is this constellation relevant for your future? What is the consequence of this special time in history for each one of you as a personality?

You can utilize the special energy that is available to you now, to choose peace, love and harmony over the old programs of lower emotions such as ego-based fears, control and manipulation. Many of you have chosen this unique opportunity on earth to witness the turning point in history. So, what advantage does your being here now have for you?

Each of you has a past, present and future history of millions of existing consciousnesses. I'm sure that you have heard before that time does not exist. But what does that really mean? Why is it so important to understand time and the purpose it was created for?

Time exists for the sole purpose of giving us focus. You could say time is the program, the tool you can use, to organize the chain of events you have chosen to live, in order to understand and learn from the choices you make.

Time is a positive blockage! Without time, a successive chain of actions and reactions, you would not understand the consequences of your thoughts, feelings and actions. Without time you would have no framework to 'begin' and 'end' certain phases of your development, you would have no goal and you would have great difficulties accomplishing a greater purpose.

The timeline and consequential chain of events make it possible for us to focus on each period and live that experience before moving on to the next more advanced experience. That way, for instance, you can feel and understand the vast subject of relationships and communication as a child, further as an adolescent, later as an adult. Each cycle of time will allow you to perceive these themes with new meaning.

These conclusions, which are derived throughout many experiences, make up the composition of your personality, with which you make further choices. Each commitment you make describes who you are and who you choose to be in fullest detail. Time connects all events and makes it possible for you to succeed and transcend each occurrence, selecting exactly what defines you.

The earth's consciousness is preparing for an evolutionary step towards selecting its true identity. This selection is similar to the lifelong process of elimination that makes it evident what is important to you and what is not. In this time of history, the earth, which is bound to universal evolution, will shed its old pool of events and materalize its new goals. The earth will express peace, love and harmony over fear-based ego programs. How can the earth choose? Does the earth have a mind?

The earth is a living being that has 'commited' to house and support you for your life experiences. The basis for this 'choice' is its empathy for all living beings. Many cultures regard the earth as our mother and appreciate the gift of life it has given.

But the most amazing change that will take place within the next decade is the earth's evolution toward developing its 'mind', and to consequentially favor peace and harmony over war and manipulation. The earth has long begun to weed out its old patterns of living and housing conflict and oppression, of allowing destruction and suppression. The earth will successively sustain love over hate, light over darkness, its ultimate godlike potential over limitation.

You are here to benefit from this cleansing process. You can elevate your frequencies, take part in this deep and thorough process, choose light over darkness, consciousness over illusion, etc. in all your decisions, actions and reactions. This is one of the greater gifts that is in store for you, if you choose to be a part of it.

The following manifestations are meant as a tool to transform the illusions of your past into the freedom and power of truth, clarity and justice.

The 'demonic' program on earth has been created to help us reflect, gain insight and grow in every facet of our being. Polarity helps to clarify your personal truths and untruths.

Often you have made diplomatic choices, so as not to jeopardize your position, for instance out of fear of losing what you have achieved. These fears have kept you bound, through the laws of attraction, with authorities who suppressed you for their own purpose. You were not free to live your higher potential. To free yourself from these dependencies, you must cleanse yourself of all existing fears, limitations and experiences, where you have chosen dark over light, illusion over truth, manipulation over love.

You have little time to free yourselves from overwhelming patterns and emotional programs. These prayers connect you with strong light entities that support your cause, to expand your soul and mind, and choose peace and love in every cell of your being, achieving the perfect consequences of development as a divine being.

Many people will subconsciously choose not to be a part of this greater change in reality and outwardly they will deny the existence of the godlike potential in each and every living being. They will continue to accuse mankind of being bad, helpless and unworthy to keep you fearful and to manipulate you. This is not unjust! It is the reaction to your actions in thousands of lifetimes which falsely convinces you of your defenselessness and allows you to be blinded. Only your awareness, intentions and focus can heal this 'past'. It is your conviction and determination to find the truth in every illusion, and stand up for yourself and others that will change reality. These prayers are a call for help. We are ready to 'fight' for your cause whenever you call us. For you, the fighting is over. Choose peace and unite with those who do.

❧ Ridding Your Mind of ❧ Negative Thoughts

I thank you for my willingness
in every now moment
to recognize the higher good
in all situations,
destinies and coincidences.

I thank you that I am able to see
the spark of godliness
in every man and woman,
regardless of their race,
religion and faults.

I thank you that my heart is open
to the feeling of graciousness
and thankfulness for every living being
that I meet and every day that I live.

I thank you that I am free of self-pity and victimhood,
and judgement of myself and others.

I thank you for the wondrous planet earth
and all the recourses that support me
so that I may learn and grow.

God's universe is the miracle of existence.

ᢒ **Willingness to Follow** ᢒ
the Path of Light

I thank you that my inner focus
on the universal shining rays of light
is supported and intensified.

I thank you that all evidence
of wounds and pains
that distract me from God's path
is healed and forgiven.

I thank you that my ego, soul and spirit
are willing to face and clear
all discomfort and weaknesses
that have led me to darkness and manipulation.

I thank you that God's love
guides me to follow the path of passion
and purity of consciousness
and I thank you that my yearning
for God's light is strong and pure.

My path is the light of the universe.

ॐ Demonic Influences, Entities and ॐ Dark Energies in the Bodies

I thank you creator, that all
vibrations of unworthiness
that are being held
in my planes of existence
are healed and harmonized.

I thank you that
all structures of dependence,
which undermine my confidence
and joy of decision,
are filled with light and love.

I am one with all that is,
light and love in this universe,
my divine source and all my supporting beings
in the twelfth plane of existence.

I thank you that I remain free
of all discordant energy
in all cells of my existence,
in all planes of my dimensions.

☙ Demonic Influences, Entities and ❧ Dark Energies in Rooms

I thank you that all capacities
of dark entities and energies in these rooms
are dispersed, delegated and secluded.

I thank you that all rooms
are harmonized and sealed
to all discrepancies of demonic energy.

I thank you that light and dark
are in balance of truth
in every given moment,
in every given realm,
dimension and space.

Mine is the clarity and support of spiritual
growth within my surroundings.

❧ Letting Go of Dark Convictions ❧

I thank you for God's wonder
of impartial light,
which raises my level of consciousness
to the realms of heaven,
to realize and to hold
the value of everlasting
truth and compassion.

I thank you that my mind
and my whole willingness
to serve God's will of light and harmony
are elevated to the angelic realms
of joyous embrace.

I thank you that all facets of my existence
are at peace to shine in heavenly
light and benevolence.

I am fulfillment of peace and joy of
the brotherhood of light.

I thank you that all hidden convictions
of persecution and powerlessness
are cleansed within my heart and spirit.

I thank you that all residue of destruction
is erased and all emptiness is filled
with God's warm light
of forgiveness and consolation.

God is the light of my heart and soul.

৯ Letting Go of Disempowering Fears ৯

I thank you for the forfeit
of prohibited tasks
in any now of my existential beings
and for the grace of God's healing
in every dimensional plane
of my past, present and future.

I thank you that I release all destruction,
powerlessness and fear of disgrace
in the deepest fathoms of soul.

I thank you for the blessings
bestowed upon me,
which cleanse all darkness
of my inner conviction.

I thank you for the love
that flows through me
and frees me from the lowest darkness
of my heart's structure.

Mine is the glory of releasing all fears.

ॐ Sabotage through ॐ Hidden Dark Dimensions

I thank you that I may reveal
and release the hidden darkness
of my soul's inner consciousness.

I thank you that I may let my inner self
rise to my highest potential
of God's shining light.

I thank you that my false illusions
are purified with my true colors
of passion and acceptance.

I am the pure light of being.

❧ Manipulative Behavior by Way ❧ of Genetic Information

I thank you that all family ties
that flow through me and bind me
to the destructive behavior
of manipulation and exploitation
are severed and healed.

I thank you for the trust
in universal goodness
and justice that soothes my spirit
and fills my actions
with consideration and empathy.

I thank you that the wondrous qualities
of grace and love
harmonize my heart
to the godliness of mankind.

I am filled with the insight
of God's reflection.

I thank you that I am free
from all discordant energy
in every time and space,
in all my cells of existence,
in all my planes of dimension.